WARBIRDS ILLUSTRATED NO. 8

Cover illustration: This rear-threequarter view of a Tupolev Tu-26 'Backfire-B' was taken over the Baltic Sea. It shows clearly the AS-6 'Kitchen' air-to-surface missile semi-submerged into the 'Backfire's' belly, and the rear turret mounting a pair of 23mm cannon, with a 'Fan Tail' radar dish above the turret. (Flygvapnet)

1. The Ilyushin Il-76 'Candid', which bears a passing resemblance to the Starlifter, is now beginning to replace the An-12 'Cub' as the standard transport for Soviet airborne forces. This photograph shows paratroops preparing to board a 'Candid'. Note the twin 23mm NR-23 cannon in the tail turret. Some 140 'Candids' are thought to be in service with the Military Transport Aviation. (Tass)

Warsaw Pact Air Power in the 1980s

Bulgaria • Czechoslovakia • East Germany
Hungary • Poland • Romania • Soviet Union

MICHAEL J. GETHING

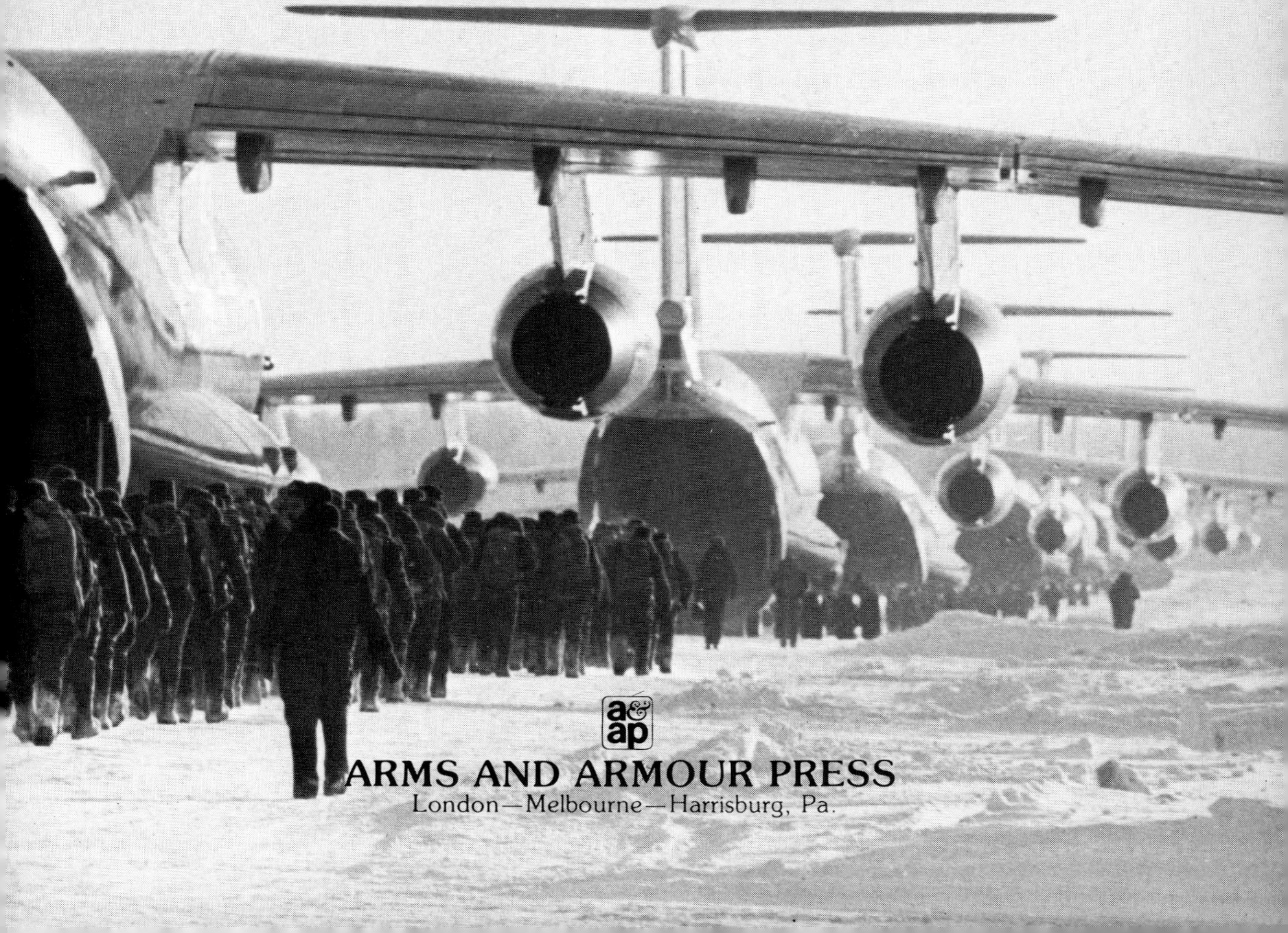

a&ap
ARMS AND ARMOUR PRESS
London—Melbourne—Harrisburg, Pa.

Introduction

Warbird 8: Warsaw Pact Air Power in the 1980s
Published in 1982 by
Arms and Armour Press, Lionel Leventhal Limited, 2–6 Hampstead High Street, London NW3 1QQ; 4–12 Tattersalls Lane, Melbourne, Victoria 3000, Australia; Cameron and Kelker Streets, PO Box 1831, Harrisburg, Pennsylvania 17105, USA.

British Library Cataloguing in Publication Data:
Gething, M. J.
Warsaw Pact air power in the 1980s. – (Warbirds illustrated; 8)
1. Warsaw Pact, 1955
2. Airplanes, Military – Pictorial works
I. Title II. Series
623.74'6'091717 UG1245.E/
ISBN 0-85368-546-0

Layout by Anthony A. Evans.
Printed in Great Britain by William Clowes (Beccles) Limited.

The publication late last year of *Soviet Military Power* by the US Department of Defense has done more to highlight the growing threat to the western world than any other document. With regard to air power, the book points out that more than 3,500 Soviet and Warsaw Pact tactical bombers and fighters are located in Eastern Europe alone. In each of the last eight years, the Soviet Union has produced more than 1,000 fighter aircraft. In excess of 5,200 helicopters are now available to the Soviet Armed Forces, including increasing numbers of Mi-8 'Hip' and Mi-24 'Hind' helicopter gunships used in direct support of ground forces on the battlefield. These statistics alone should cause the average peace-loving citizen to ponder the long-term intentions of the Soviet Union and her allies.

The Soviet Union's Air Force is divided into three distinct air arms: Frontal (or Tactical) Aviation, Long Range Aviation and Military Transport Aviation (which is backed up by the mighty Soviet airline, Aeroflot). Air defence is the responsibility of an entirely separate service, the Air Force of the Air Defence of the Homeland, and this incorporates both fighter aircraft and missile defences. In addition, there is Soviet Naval Aviation, consisting of some 1,440 aircraft and helicopters, most of which are land-based with the exception of the Yak-36 'Forger' assigned to the *Kiev* class carriers and helicopters deployed on cruisers and aircraft carriers.

Added to the Soviet air arms are the air forces of her Warsaw Pact allies: Bulgaria, Czechoslovakia, East Germany, Hungary, Poland and Romania. These air forces are primarily of a tactical nature, and are generally some five years behind the Soviet Union in terms of aircraft deployed. Of the Warsaw Pact allies, Czechoslovakia leads the 'effectiveness stakes' possessing many MiG-23 'Flogger-B' and MiG-27 'Flogger-D' aircraft.

To compile this book, many sources were tapped but it goes to Western sources to supply the major part of the book. Some photographs will be new to the reader, while others included may be the only ones available to illustrate certain types. I trust that the reader will find the resulting selection of interest. I wish to acknowledge and thank the UK Ministry of Defence, the RAF Staff College, the US Department of Defense and Captain Jan Sovjack of the Czechoslovak Embassy for their particular assistance in supplying material for inclusion in this book.

Michael J. Gething, Farnborough, 1982.

2. A Soviet pilot prepares to make a sortie in his MiG-21SMT 'Fishbed-K'. The MiG-21 series is the most widely-used fighter in the world, and has provided the main strength of the Soviet and Warsaw Pact air forces for many years. Note the two pylons under each wing with launch shoes for the K-13 (AA-2 'Atoll') air-to-air missiles (AAMs).

◀2

▲3

3. A line-up of Antonov An-12BP 'Cub-A' transport aircraft, after off-loading ASU-85 self-propelled guns of the Soviet airborne forces. Some 560 'Cub-As' are thought to be in Soviet service, although the Il-76 'Candid' is starting to replace this equivalent of the C-130 Hercules. Note the twin 23mm NR-23 cannon in the tail turret. (Tass)

4. This night shot shows an An-12BP 'Cub-A' transport taxiing out to take-off. Other versions of the 'Cub' in Soviet and Warsaw Pact service include an electronic intelligence (ELINT) version, the 'Cub-B', and some 30 electronic countermeasures (ECM) versions with an ogival tailcone replacing the tail turret, the 'Cub-C'.

5. By far the largest transport aircraft in use with Soviet forces is the Antonov An-22 'Cock', known as Antheus by the Russians. The 'Cock' first flew on 27 February 1965, and some 50 aircraft had been built by the time production stopped in 1974. With a weight (empty, equipped) of 251,325lb (114,000kg), the 'Cock' is the only Soviet transport capable of carrying a T-62 main battle tank.

4▲ 5▼

▲6

7▲

6. A military derivative of the Il-18 airliner is the Il-38 'May' maritime reconnaissance and anti-submarine warfare (ASW) aircraft – whose development was similar in a way to that of the US Lockheed Orion which was born of the Electra airliner – with a slightly lengthened fuselage, an undernose radome and a magnetic anomaly detection (MAD) 'sting' in the tail. About 60 'Mays' are thought to be in Soviet Naval Air Force service. This photograph shows an A-7E Corsair from the USS *Nimitz* escorting a 'May' over the Indian Ocean in April 1980. (US Navy)

7. Although basically a passenger airliner of Britannia vintage which serves with Aeroflot, the Ilyushin Il-18 has been developed for two military roles. This photograph shows the Il-18 'Coot-A' ECM/ELINT version, which was identified for the first time in 1978. The large canoe-shaped pod beneath the fuselage is thought to house a sideways-looking radar, while other blisters and pods contain sensors of various types. (RAF)

8. This Beriev Be-12 'Mail' amphibious maritime patrol aircraft, known as the M-12 Tchaika (Seagull) by the Russians, replaced the earlier piston-engined Be-6. Powered by a pair of Ivchenko AI-20D turboprops, rated at 4,190ehp, the 'Mail' entered Soviet Naval Air Force service in the mid-1960s. (Tass)

8▼

9. This photograph of the An-22 'Cock', taken during the 'West-81' series of military exercises, shows the air-dropping of a BMD infantry combat vehicle of the Soviet airborne forces. The maximum payload of the 'Cock' is 176,350lb (80,000kg). (Tass)
10. This Antonov An-26 'Curl' transport, photographed during the Paris air show in 1979, is developed from the An-24RT 'Coke' transport, but equipped with a new rear fuselage of the 'beaver-tail' type and powered by a pair of Ivchenko AI-24T turboprops, rated at 2,820ehp. It is generally used as a cargo aircraft by Aeroflot, the Soviet airline, but can easily be converted for paratrooping or casualty-evacuation duties. (MJG)
11. An Antonov An-26 'Curl' transport of the Yugoslav Air Force, which although not strictly part of the Warsaw Pact remains still within the Soviet sphere of influence. (via UK MoD)
12. The Antonov An-28 'Cash' was developed to replace the An-14 'Clod', and is understood to have made its maiden flight in September 1969. This photograph shows the second development aircraft, which is powered by a pair of Glushenkov TBD-10B turboprops, rated at 960shp. Production of this general-purpose transport is now undertaken by WSK-PZL Mielec in Poland. (Tass)

11▲ 12▼

▲13 ▼14

13. The Antonov An-30 'Clank', the first specialized aerial survey aircraft to be developed by the Soviet Union. This photograph, taken at the Hanover air show in 1974, clearly shows the glazed nose and increased height of the flight deck. The 'Clank' is developed from the An-24 'Coke'. (MJG)

14. This Antonov An-32 'Cline' short-medium range transport was developed from the An-26 'Curl' transport for use in high altitude or high temperature environments. Although similar to the 'Curl', it has enlarged ventral fins and a full-span slotted tail-plane, and is powered by a pair of Ivchenko AI-20M turboprops, rated at 5,180ehp. This photograph was taken at the Paris air show in 1977. (MJG)

15. The similarity between the Boeing YC-14 Advanced Medium STOL Transport prototype and this Antonov An-72 'Coaler' jet transport is obvious. Powered by a pair of Lotarev D-36 high-bypass turbofans, rated at 14,330lb st, and using the 'Coanda effect' over the extended flaps, a high degree of lift may be obtained. The military potential of this aircraft lies in its ability to use natural landing fields or small airfields. It could even be used to support V/STOL operations by the successor to the Yak-36 'Forger'. This aircraft was photographed during the 1981 Paris air show. (MJG)
16. An Il-76 'Candid' at the Paris air show in 1981. Note the two nose radomes: the nose tip radome houses a weather radar, while the undernose radome houses a ground-mapping radar. It is known that a tanker version of the 'Candid' has been developed for support of the Tu-26 'Backfire' fleet in both Soviet Long Range Aviation and Naval Air Force service, while an airborne warning and control system version (AWACS) is also under development. (MJG)

15▲ 16▼

▲17 ▼18

19▲

17. The Ilyushin Il-86 'Camber' was the Soviets' first wide-body jet transport. It made its maiden flight on 22 December, 1976. Powered by four Kuznetsov NK-86 turbofans, rated at 28,660lb st each, the 'Camber' is basically a civil airliner, although in the event of hostilities it would be used for military purposes. This photograph was taken during the 1981 Paris air show. (MJG)
18. The Kamov Ka-25 'Hormone-A' is the Soviet Navy's standard ASW helicopter, deployed aboard the VTOL carriers *Kiev* and *Minsk*, the helicopter cruisers *Moskva* and *Leningrad* and various *Kresta* and *Kara* class guided-missile cruisers. Powered by a pair of Glushenkov GTD-3 turboshaft engines, each rated at 900shp, the 'Hormone' has a configuration not unlike the American Huskie helicopter. Apart from ASW work, it is understood the 'Hormone' is used for mid-course guidance of anti-shipping missiles, and this version is designated 'Hormone-B'. This photograph shows a 'Hormone-A' overflying the Royal Navy's vessel HMS *Ark Royal* during Exercise Ocean Safari 1975.
19. Ka-25 'Hormone-A' ASW helicopters landing on one of the Soviet Navy's helicopter cruisers, either *Moskva* or *Leningrad*. Note the undernose radome, housing a search radar; and the anti-skid nets on the deck landing spots. (via UK MoD)
20. This photograph shows a new version of the Kamov Ka-25 'Hormone' ASW helicopter, during trials with the Soviet destroyer *Udaloy* in the Baltic Sea. The new helicopter is codenamed 'Helix', and features an enlarged cabin and strengthened horizontal stabilizer with twin fins.

20▼

▲21

21. Although the first prototype version of the MiG-21 'Fishbed' flew on 16 June 1956, and was a day fighter of limited range, the series has been progressively developed over the years into a multi-mission all-weather fighter. It has been supplied to many countries outside the Soviet Union and Warsaw Pact, and is thought to be the most widely-used fighter in the world. This photograph shows the first production version, the MiG-21F 'Fishbed-C', armed with two 30mm NR-30 cannon and provision for a pair of K-13/AA-2 'Atoll' IR-homing air-to-air missiles, of the Czech Air Force deploying its brake parachute on landing.

22. This MiG-21MF 'Fishbed-J' is generally similar to the MiG-21PFMA 'Fishbed-J', the first multi-mission version in the series. Re-engined with a Tumansky R-13-300 turbojet, rated at 11,240lb st (dry) and 14,550lb st (with reheat), it is lighter than the 'Fishbed-J' and has a higher performance. The 'Fishbed-J' entered Soviet service in 1970. (Tass)

23. In 1978, six MiG-23S 'Flogger-G' fighters made goodwill visits to France and Finland. These aircraft differed from the standard 'Flogger-B' version in having practically no operational equipment. It may be that a small batch of aircraft have been modified thus as demonstration aircraft. (J. M. Guhl)

24. The MiG-21 is probably the best known of Soviet fighters. This photograph shows the MiG-21PFMA 'Fishbed-J' multi-mission fighter variant. The deep dorsal fairing contains fuel tankage and, although seen here with underwing fuel tanks, four 'Atoll' air-to-air missiles are usually carried. The centreline fuel tank is more common, although there is provision for a GP-9 underbelly gun pack. (via US DoD)

▼22

▲23 ▼24

▲25

▲26 ▼27

28▲

25. The Sukhoi Su-7B 'Fitter-A' is an important part of the Polski Wojska Lotnicze, where they are assigned to a tactical support role. Armed with two 30mm NR-30 cannon in the wing roots, and four underwing and two underfuselage pylons, the 'Fitter-A' is an effective aircraft. Note the bulge under the lower fuselage below the cockpit: this is probably a fairing on the nose undercarriage door, rather than a laser rangefinder. (via US DoD)
26. Poland also has a number of Sukhoi Su-20 'Fitter-Cs' on strength. The Su-20 is an 'export' version of the Su-17 'Fitter-C', with a lower rated engine and a change of internal avionics equipment. The Su-17/20 is itself a variable-geometry version of the Su-7, with the sweep in the outer panels only. Probably most of the Su-7B 'Fitter-As' in Polish service are being replaced by the Su-20 'Fitter C'. (via US DoD)
27. Three Su-15s, probably the 'Flagon-E' variant with uprated engines, each armed with a pair of AA-3 'Anab' missiles. These aircraft are gradually being replaced by MiG-23 'Flogger-B' and MiG-25 'Foxbat-A' interceptors; but even so, at the end of 1981, some 700 'Flagons' were thought to be still in service. (via UK MoD)
28. A group of Soviet pilots returning to the crewroom after a sortie. The aircraft shown are the single-seat MiG-21SMT 'Fishbed-K' (with a deeper dorsal spine extended rearwards) and the two-seat MiG-21UM 'Mongol-B' trainer. (Tass)
29. This photograph of a MiG-21SMT 'Fishbed-K' taxiing clearly shows the extended and deeper dorsal spine, which provides increased fuel capacity and optimum aerodynamic form. Like the 'Fishbed-J' models, it can carry both the K-13A 'Atoll' IR-homing AAMs or the radar-homing 'Advanced Atolls'. There is also provision for detachable ECM pods on the wing-tips. Delivery of this model to Warsaw Pact air forces is thought to have begun in 1971. (Tass)

29▼

22726
22722
22724
723

726
13

▲31

30. (on previous spread) The second major production version of the MiG-21 was the MiG-21PF 'Fishbed-D', with a less tapered forward fuselage and enlarged air intake to house the R1L 'Spin Scan A' radar in the nose cone. This photograph shows a group of Yugoslav Air Force pilots about to board their 'Fishbed-Ds'.

31. The MiG-21bis 'Fishbed-L' shown here is the third generation of MiG-21. It is configured for the multi-mission, air combat/ground-attack role with updated avionics and generally improved standards of construction. Careful observation of the underwing stores shows an air-to-ground rocket pod on the inner pylon, while there appears to be a light 500kg bomb on the outer pylon. (Tass)

32. The MiG-21bis 'Fishbed-N' is an advanced version of the 'Fishbed-L', re-engined with the Tumansky R-25 turbojet rated at 16,535lb st with reheat. The radar detection range of this model is thought to be 18.5 miles (30km), and the armament consists of two AA-8 'Aphid' IR-homing AAMs on the inboard pylons and two AA-2-2 'Advanced Atoll' radar-homing AAMs on the outer pylons. (via US DoD)

33. Deployment of the Soviet Union's first variable-geometry air combat fighter, the MiG-23 'Flogger', is thought to have begun in 1973, and by 1981 over 2,000 aircraft are thought to have been built. This photograph shows the basic MiG-23MF 'Flogger-B', which has now replaced the MiG-21 as the primary air-to-air tactical fighter of the Soviet Air Forces. This version is also in service with Czechoslovakia, East Germany and Hungary, and has been exported to nine other air forces. (via UK MoD)

32▲ 33▼

▲34 ▼35

34. This recently-released photograph shows a camouflaged MiG-23MF 'Flogger-B' of the Soviet Frontal Aviation during their Exercise West-81 in September 1981. The 'Flogger-B' is powered by a Tumanksy R-29B turbojet, rated at 25,350lb st (with reheat), and fitted with triple stores ejection racks on the wing glove pylon. Note also the laser rangefinder under the forward fuselage aft of the 'High Lark' radome. (Tass)

35. This MiG-23MF 'Flogger-B' of the Czech Air Force is clearly configured for the air combat role. Note the two K-13A 'Atoll' AAMs on the underfuselage pylons, and the launch shoes on the glove pylons, presumably for the AA-7 'Apex' semi-active radar-homing AAMs. Also visible are the reheat pressure cones in the jet efflux, and also the leading edge flaps on the outer (variable-geometry) wing panels.

36, 37. During 1978, six MiG-23MFs paid a courtesy visit to France from the Soviet air base of Kubinka. These aircraft featured a smaller dorsal fin than the standard 'Flogger-B', together with an absence of stores pylons and laser rangefinder. This suggests that a few aircraft have been modified to allow a greater aerobatic performance for use as a display team. This version has been re-designated 'Flogger-G' by NATO, and has since been identified with a new sensor pod, and so is considered an operational type. The smaller dorsal fin is clearly visible (**37**), as are the reheat pressure cones in the jet efflux.

36▲ 37▼

▲38 ▼39

38. A MiG-23MF 'Flogger-B' all-weather air combat fighter of the Soviet Air Force, seen here armed with AA-7 'Apex' semi-active radar-homing AAMs on the wing glove pylons and AA-8 'Aphid' IR-homing AAMs on the underfuselage pylons. The 'Flogger-B' is reported to be the first Soviet aircraft to have demonstrated its ability to track and engage targets flying below its own altitude. (via US DoD)

39. This view of a 'Flogger-G' landing during its visit to France clearly shows the brake parachute, and the spindly undercarriage. The only stores pylon visible is the centreline station, which carried fuel tanks for the transit flight to France. (SIRPA)

▲40

40. Apart from its use as a high-altitude interceptor, the MiG-25 has also been developed into an effective reconnaissance aircraft. This photograph shows the MiG-25R 'Foxbat-B' reconnaissance version with underfuselage camera ports and nose-mounted dielectric panels for the smaller nose radar and sideways-looking airborne radar (SLAR). Thought to have entered Soviet service in 1971, the 'Foxbat-B' has also been exported to Algeria, Libya and Syria, and eight are in the process of delivery to the Indian Air Force. (via US DoD)

41. Initially designed to counter the US B-70 Valkyrie supersonic bomber (cancelled in 1961), the MiG-25 'Foxbat' is a Mach 3 high altitude interceptor. For this role, it is armed with four AA-6 'Acrid' AAMs, two of which are equipped with IR-homing heads and two with radar-homing heads. The wing-tip fairings visible in this photograph are thought to house the continuous-wave target illuminating equipment for the radar-homing 'Acrids'. The 'Foxbat' was described in 1973 by the-then US Secretary of the Air Force, Dr. Robert C. Seamans, as 'probably the best interceptor in production in the world today'. (via US DoD)

42. One of the first Soviet-released photographs of the 'Foxbat', showing two versions of the MiG-25R. The differing nose radome sizes and dielectric panels for the SLAR are clearly visible. The aircraft in the foreground is definitely the 'Foxbat-B', with the bulged housing under the nose thought to contain the ground-mapping radar and Doppler antennae. The other aircraft is probably the 'Foxbat-D' with a slightly larger SLAR dielectric panel further aft than on the 'Foxbat-B'. (Tass)

41▲ 42▼

43. The ground crew of this Czech MiG-23BN 'Flogger-F' are apparently making some minor adjustments to the aircraft, prior to a night sortie. The 'anchor'-like object to the left of the aircraft would appear to be a stores trolley of some description.
44. Although at first sight, this 'Flogger' appears to be the MiG-27 –D version, it is actually a MiG-23BN 'Flogger-F'. Although retaining the nose shape and equipment of the 'Flogger-D', it has the variable intake of the MiG-23, with the 23mm GSh-23 twin barrel cannon and Tumansky R-29B turbojet. Again note the folded ventral fin in this landing shot. (Tass)
45. The dedicated ground-attack version of the MiG-23 is designated MiG-27 'Flogger-D', and although similar in many respects, there are some important differences. It features fixed air intakes and nozzle for high subsonic speeds at low altitude, a sharply-tapering nose with a small window for a laser rangefinder and marked targer seeker, and a six-barrelled 23mm rotary cannon. This 1976 photograph of a 'Flogger-D' clearly shows the larger, low-pressure tyres and the ventral fin in the folded position for landing. (via UK MoD)

▼43

44▲ 45▼

46. Another shot of the MiG-23BN 'Flogger-F', proclaimed by the variable-geometry intakes. The window for the laser range-finder and marked target seeker is clearly visible on the upturn of the nose, as are the low-pressure tyres. Although this model is ostensibly for export, the 'Flogger-F' has been placed in Soviet Frontal Aviation service. (Tass)

47. This view of a Czech Air Force MiG-23BN 'Flogger-F', taken during Exercise Druzba '79, apparently shows a pilot waiting on quick reaction alert; witness the two electric cables hanging from the nose section of the aircraft. The small blister just above the front of the nose-wheel door is an antenna for the 'Sirena 3' radar warning system. As both groundcrewmen are carrying satchels of some description, it is possible they are in a form of partial NBC (nuclear, chemical and biological) protection suit: the satchels holding their gas masks.

▲46 ▼47

48▲ 49▼

48. This Mil Mi-2 'Hoplite' helicopter, seen here liaising with a troop of T-62 tanks, has been built by WSK-PZL Swidnik in Poland since 1964. More than 3,000 examples of the 'Hoplite' have been produced in 24 versions (both civil and military) since then, with over 2,000 going to the Soviet Union. Apart from military liaison duties, the 'Hoplite' can be armed with four AT-3 'Sagger' anti-tank missiles, this version serving with the Polish Army. (via UK MoD)

49. Looking not unlike the Sikorsky S.55 Whirlwind, the Mil Mi-4 'Hound' was one of the first Soviet transport and ASW helicopters, and has since been largely replaced by the Mi-8 'Hip'. However, as this Czech Air Force example illustrates, it is still in limited use within the Warsaw Pact. The aircraft shown here features an underfuselage pod, which could contain either an air-to-ground cannon (unlikely) or some form of ECM equipment. If it is the latter, then the NATO codename is 'Hound-C'.

▲50 ▼51

50. Soviet airborne forces (including a mortar crew) landing from a Mil Mi-6 'Hook' heavy general-purpose helicopter. The 'Hook' was first announced in 1957. Ten years later a fire-fighting version was demonstrated at the Paris air show. Over 800 'Hooks' are known to have been built. (Tass)
51. This photograph, released in mid-1981, shows a pair of Mil Mi-6 'Hooks' of the Soviet Navy carrying Russian Marines during an amphibious landing. The 'Hook' has been widely exported within and beyond Warsaw Pact nations. (Tass)
52. The Tu-26 'Backfire-B' (referred to by President Brezhnev as the Tu-22M during the SALT talks) is the only long-range bomber in production in the Soviet Union. Some 150 aircraft are believed to be in service, divided equally between the Aviatsiya Dal'nevo Deistviya (Long Range Aviation) and Aviatsiya veonno-morskovo Flota (Naval Aviation), and this number is increasing at the rate of 30+ per year. The 'Backfire-B' is capable of flying at Mach 2.5 and can carry nuclear or conventional bombs or air-to-surface missiles. (Flygvapnet)
53. The interception of Soviet long-range maritime patrol or reconnaissance aircraft is almost an everyday occurrence for the USAF and RAF in Europe. This photograph, however, shows an interception of a Tupolev Tu-95 'Bear-D' of Naval Aviation over the Western Pacific by a USAF F-15 Eagle. Some 45 'Bear-Ds' are understood to be in use to provide mid-course corrections for surface-to-surface and air-to-surface missiles. (USAF)

52▲ 53▼

▲54 ▼55

56▲

54. Although seen here in civil Aeroflot markings, the Ilyushin Il-76T 'Candid' is an important part of the Voenno-transportnaya Aviatsiya (Air Transport Aviation). The 'Candid' entered service in 1974, and about 75 are thought to be in use. Development of a tanker version (to refuel 'Backfire') is understood to be under way. (via US DoD)
55. This Aérospatiale/Westland IAR.330 Puma of the Romanian forces is an unusual aircraft to be found within the context of the Warsaw Pact. Romania has built 90 Pumas under licence and, as this photograph shows, has armed them with air-to-ground rocket pods. (Viara Militara)
56. The 'Hip-E' version of the Mil Mi-8 helicopter, landing Border Guards to investigate an incident (according to the caption). The 'Hip-E' is probably one of the most heavily-armed Soviet helicopters. Apart from the nose-mounted 12.7mm machine-gun, its stores pylons can carry six rocket pods (with a total of 192 air-to-ground rockets) and four AT-2 'Swatter' anti-tank missiles. (Tass)
57. Using the Mi-6 'Hook' as a starting point, the Soviet Union developed a flying crane capable of carrying a platform-mounted payload of 33,070lb (15,000kg) below its fuselage. Designated Mi-10 'Harke', this helicopter was publicly unveiled at the Tushino air show in 1961. Although basically a civil helicopter, several are known to be in service with the Soviet armed forces. (Tass)

57▼

▲58

▲59 ▼60

58. The new shore-based Soviet Navy anti-submarine helicopter, the Mil Mi-14, appropriately code named 'Haze'. Developed from the Mi-8 'Hip', it features a boat-hull planing bottom, with rear-mounted sponson, similar to the Sea King. There is an under-fuselage search radar, and a towed MAD 'bird' is mounted on the rear of the fuselage.
59. Shown for the first time at the Paris air show in 1981, this Mil Mi-17 is a developed version of the Mi-8 'Hip', which it will probably replace in military service. Powered by the same engines as the Mi-14 'Haze', a pair of Isotov TV3-117MT turboshafts, each rated at 1,900shp, it has shorter engine nacelles. Note also that the lengthened fuel sponson on the starboard side has a small intake, presumably for an auxiliary power unit (APU) to assist in off-base operations. (MJG)
60. The latest helicopter to emerge from the Mil stable is this Mi-26 'Halo', which was first shown in public at the Paris air show in 1981. Developed to replace both the Mi-6 'Hook' and Mi-10 'Harke', the 'Halo' is powered by a pair of Lotarev D-136 free-turbine turboshaft engines, each rated at 11,400shp, and driving an eight-bladed rotor. Although exhibited in Aeroflot markings, the military applications of the 'Halo' are obvious, and it should not be too long before we see military versions in service. (MJG)

61▲ 62▼

61. The first major production version of the Mil Mi-24 armed assault helicopter, codenamed 'Hind-A'. Deployed into Eastern Europe in 1974, the 'Hind-A' carries a crew of four (pilot, co-pilot, navigator-gunner and forward observer) plus provision for a squad of eight troops. Its stub wings allow the carriage of four UB-32 rocket pods and four AT-2 'Swatter' anti-tank missiles. A 12.7mm machine-gun is also carried in an undernose turret. (via UK MoD)

62. This Soviet-released photograph shows several Mi-24 'Hind-As' deploying troops during a military exercise. The 'Hind-A' is powered by a pair of Isotov TV3-117 turboshaft engines, each with a maximum rating of 2,200shp. Shown here are both the early production version with the starboard-side tail rotor (in the air) and the later version with a port-mounted tail rotor (in the left foreground, and background). (Tass)

▲63 ▼64

65▲

63. The later version of the Mi-24, the 'Hind-D' with its completely re-designed nose to accommodate the weapons operator in the front with the pilot in a raised seat behind. Designed primarily for the gunship role, the single, nose gun has been replaced by a four-barrel 12.7mm rotary machine-gun. The radar and low-light television sensors have also been nose-mounted. (Tass)
64. An Mi-24 'Hind-D' in Czech service, clearly showing the re-designed nose profile for gunship use. Note the sensor pod under the forward fuselage, and the deflector plates forward of the air intakes to prevent ingestion of dust and foreign objects.
65. This head-on view shows the 'Hind-E' version of the Mi-24, which differs from the 'Hind-D' by having the new tube-launched AT-6 'Spiral' anti-tank missiles in place of the AT-2 'Swatter' missiles. The 'Hind-E' has also been structurally strengthened by substituting titanium and steel in previously aluminium-constructed components. More than 100 'Hind-Es' are reported to be deployed in forward areas in Eastern Europe. (via US DoD)

▲66 ▼67

68▲ 69▼

66. A Myasishev M-4 'Bison', developed initially as a strategic bomber (entering service in the mid-1950s), but subsequently converted to the maritime reconnaissance and airborne tanker roles. It is estimated that only about 50 'Bisons' remain in service, most in the tanker configuration. This photograph shows the 'Bison-C' version with a revised nose profile and in-flight refuelling probe. (via US DoD)
67. The M-4 'Bison-B' maritime reconnaissance bomber. Only a few of these Mikulin AM-3D turbojet-powered aircraft remain in service. (RAF)
68. This version of the 'Fitter-A' was developed for use from short, unprepared fields. Designated Su-7BMK, it is similar to the Su-7BM, but with provision for JATO (jet assisted take-off) bottles under the rear fuselage, and a low-pressure nose-wheel tyre which required a blister in the nose-wheel undercarriage door to enclose it. This feature can be seen clearly in this photograph. Note also the MiG-23BN 'Flogger-F' in the background, which might suggest that the type may be replacing the 'Fitters' of that unit.
69. Su-7BM 'Fitter-As' shortly after take-off. Until the arrival of the MiG-23/27 and Su-17/20/22 series of tactical strike fighters in the early 1970s, the Sukhoi Su-7 'Fitter' was the Warsaw Pact's standard fighter-bomber. The endurance of the 'Fitter-A' is limited, so one invariably sees twin fuel tanks mounted on the fuselage pylons, leaving only the wing stations for weapons. It is thought that some 200 remain in Soviet Air Force service. (Tass)

▲70 ▼71

70. By way of contrast, this 'Fitter-A' is a Su-7BKL of the Czech Air Force. Note the ribbon-type brake parachute attached under the rear fuselage: the Su-7BM and BMK versions have twin brake 'chutes housed in a fairing beneath the rudder. 'Fitter-As' of all versions have been widely exported to Warsaw Pact members and nine other countries.

71. This photograph is interesting in as much as the Su-7BKL depicted is landing on the grass at the side of the runway. This version is not specifically developed for short-field performance from unmetalled strips, so one may speculate whether a genuine emergency has occurred, or the Czech equivalent of a TACEVAL has declared the runway unserviceable.

72. The twin brake parachutes of the Su-7BM 'Fitter-A' and the airbreaks on the rear fuselage are clearly visible here. It is interesting to note that the fuel tanks have been located on the inner wing pylons, and not on the fuselage pylons as is usually the case. Apart from underwing and fuselage weapons, the 'Fitter-A' is armed with a pair of 30mm NR-30 cannon in the leading edges of the wing root.

72▼

▲73 ▼74

73. The Sukhoi Su-9 'Fishpot-B' was the first supersonic interceptor in Soviet Air Force service with a limited all-weather capability. It is thought to have entered service in 1959, and was armed with four AA-1 'Alkali' AAMs directed by the R1L 'Spin Scan' S-band radar. This photograph shows the Su-9 'Fishpot-B' version.

74. Three Su-9 'Fishpot-B' interceptors being prepared for flight. The Su-9 is powered by a Lyulka AL-7F turbojet, rated at 19,840lb st with reheat. The tailed delta configuration, similar to the MiG-21, is clearly visible here. (via US DoD)

75▲ 76▼

75. In the same way as the MiG-21 series evolved, so the Su-9 became the Su-11 'Fishpot-C'. It featured an uprated Lyulka AL-7F-1 turbojet, rated at 22,046lb st with reheat, and one IR-homing and one radar-homing AA-3 'Anab' AAM as standard armament, with an Uragan 5B 'Spin Skip' X-band radar. (via UK MoD)
76. The Sukhoi Su-15 'Flagon' is a twin-jet (Tumansky R-11F2-300s, each rated 13,668lb st with reheat) delta-wing fighter with Mach 2.5 performance. (via UK MoD)

▲77

77. A clear view of the intake of the Su-17, probably a 'Fitter-H' or -'J', with the SRD-5M 'High Fix' radar in the intake centre-body and, in the window below this, a laser target seeker. Note that the Soviet aircrew use the universal language of the hands to illustrate a point on keeping formation. (Tass)

78. The Su-7 'Fitter' series has been developed to produce a variable-geometry strike fighter, re-designated Su-17 'Fitter-C'. As this photograph shows, the wing sweep is on the outer wing panels only, with the weapons pylons on the fuselage and fixed inboard part of the wing. The fixed armament of two 30mm NR-30 cannon, with 70 rounds per gun, is retained in the wing roots. (via UK MoD)

79. Two Su-17 'Fitters': the 'Fitter-G' two-seat trainer (right) and the single-seat 'Fitter-J', which can be distinguished by its angular fin and shallow ventral fin. This particular aircraft appears to have a third set of weapons pylons mounted between the inner and outer wing pylons. (Tass)

78▲ 79▼

▲80

80. This underside view of the Su-24 'Fencer' clearly shows the variable-geometry of the wings, and the first-known pivoting stores pylons on a Soviet aircraft. Note also the unusual position of the airbrakes on the forward part of the underfuselage. The 'Fencer' is credited with a combat range (hi-lo-hi) of 1,115 miles (1,800km) armed with 4,400lb (2,000kg) of weapons and two external fuel tanks. (via UK MoD)

81. Referred to by American Intelligence as 'the first modern Soviet fighter to be developed specifically as a fighter-bomber for the ground-attack mission', the Sukhoi Su-24 'Fencer' is a potent weapons system. The 'Fencer' entered service in December 1974, and by 1981 some 400 were operational in Eastern Europe. The 'Fencer' is armed with one internal gun, and can carry approximately 17,635lb (8,000kg) of weapons on its eight weapons pylons. (via US DoD)

82. The Tupolev Tu-16 'Badger' series of bombers entered series production in 1953, and nearly 2,000 were built, of which half are estimated to be in operation in one of the several versions built. This 1963 photograph shows the 'Badger-F' version, which is derived from the basic 'Badger-A' strategic bomber, but fitted with cameras in the bomb-bay and ELINT pods under the wing. (via US DoD)

81▲ 82▼

▲83

83. A pair of 'Badger-F' bombers demonstrating the unique Soviet method of wing-tip to wing-tip in-flight refuelling. It would appear that the upper aircraft is the tanker aircraft, and the lower one the receiver. Some 90 tanker conversions of various marks of Tu-16 'Badger' are thought to have been made. (Tass)

84. Only some 250 Tupolev Tu-22 'Blinder' reconnaissance bombers are thought to have been built. The type entered service in the mid-1960s, and this photograph shows the 'Blinder-B' version, with the semi-retractable in-flight refuelling probe clearly visible over the enlarged nose radar. Although designed to carry the AS-4 'Kitchen' anti-shipping missile, this is not visible in this photograph. (Tass)

▼84

85. The maritime reconnaissance version of the Tu-22 is codenamed the 'Blinder-C'. Note that the nose radar is not housed within a complete radome, and that six camera ports are located in the weapons bay. The 'Blinder' is provided with a radar-controlled tail barbette turret housing a single 23mm NR-23 cannon. (via UK MoD)
86. The trainer version of the Tu-22, codenamed 'Blinder-D' with a second cockpit located above the main cockpit. 'Blinders' are also in service with Libya and Iraq.

85▲ 86▼

▲87

87. A Tu-22 'Blinder-C' taking off. Note the large slab flaps in use and the tail-mounted engines, which are thought to be Kolesov VD-7, each rated at 31,000lb (14,000kg). (Tass)

88. This photograph, taken on the same sortie as illustration 89, shows the underside of the Tu-142 'Bear-F' ASW aircraft. The underbelly radome is slightly smaller than on the 'Bear-D' and is positioned farther forward, while the bulged nose-wheel doors would indicate the use of low-pressure tyres on the undercarriage. The 'Bear-F' was first identified in 1973, and some 40 were thought to be operational by 1981. (via UK MoD)

89. The Tu-142 'Bear-F' is a much-refined anti-submarine version of the 'Bear', with a larger, lengthened fairing aft of the inboard engine nacelles. The ventral gun position has been replaced by a second weapons bay, leaving the tail turret with two 23mm NR-23 cannon as the sole defensive armament. Note the nose refuelling probe, which indicates the Soviet use of probe-and-drogue air-to-air refuelling. (via UK MoD)

88▲ 89▼

▲90 ▼91

92▲

90. The long range and endurance of the Tupolev Tu-95/142 'Bear' series are thought to be the main attributes that have kept the aircraft in Soviet service for over 25 years. It was revealed during the SALT negotiations in 1979 that the Soviet Air Force fleet of 'Bear-A/B' bombers are designated Tu-95, while the 75 'Bears' of the Soviet Naval Air Force are designated Tu-142. This photograph shows a Tu-142 'Bear-D', which is used to locate targets for surface-to-surface and air-to-surface anti-shipping missiles and provide mid-course guidance for them. (Peter Stevenson, UK MoD)

91. The first interception of a Soviet aircraft – a Tu-142 'Bear-D' – by the Fleet Air Arm's Sea Harrier FRS.1. The interception, by 801 Naval Air Squadron flying from HMS *Invincible*, occurred in August 1981 during Exercise Ocean Venture, some 700 miles from the Greenland/Iceland gap. The large underbelly radome on the 'Bear-D' is thought to contain an X-band radar. (801 Naval Air Sqn.)

92. The first generation of Soviet airborne warning and control system (AWACS) aircraft, the Tupolev Tu-126 'Moss', derived from the Tu-114 'Cleat' airliner. Intended to work with interceptors, the 'Moss' directs them against incoming targets, which they attack with 'snap-down' air-to-air missiles. US Department of Defense sources rate the 'Moss' ineffective over land, but capable of operations over sea. (via UK MoD)

93. A good view of the rotodome housing the AEW radar on the Tu-126 'Moss'. Note also the small blisters around the rear fuselage. It is known that at least ten 'Moss' are in Soviet Air Force service, and that a development of the Il-76 'Candid' is under way to replace the 'Moss' in the AWACS role. (USAF)

93▼

▲94 ▼95

94. Although referred to by President Brezhnev as the Tu-22M, it is thought that the Tupolev 'Backfire' variable-geometry bomber is designated Tu-26. This photograph, taken by the Royal Swedish Air Force (Flygvapnet) over the Baltic Sea in 1979, shows the 'Backfire-B' version, armed with an AS-4 'Kitchen' anti-shipping missile under the belly of the aircraft. (Flygvapnet)

95. The largest interceptor in Soviet service is this Tupolev Tu-28P 'Fiddler', referred to as the Tu-128 by the US Department of Defense. This photograph shows a 'Fiddler' armed with four AA-5 'Ash' AAMs, two being of the IR-homing variety, and two being guided by the aircraft's 'Big Nose' radar. (US DoD via *Jane's All the World's Aircraft*)

96. The crew of a Tu-28P 'Fiddler' discussing their mission prior to take-off. The 'Fiddler', of which 130 are thought to remain in service, is due to be replaced by an improved version of the MiG-25 'Foxbat'. Note the eleven 'red stars' below the cockpit, which although an unlikely record of 'kills', may well record successful 'operational' interceptions. (Tass)

96▼

▲97 ▼98

97. The Yakovlev Yak-28P 'Firebar' is a two-seat all-weather fighter, developed from the Yak-28 'Brewer' bomber. It is armed with two AA-3 'Anab' AAMs (not shown in this photograph). Some 300 of the 'Firebar' version remain in Soviet service. (via UK MoD)
98. The trainer version of the Yak-28 'Brewer'/'Firebar', codenamed 'Maestro' by NATO and designated Yak-28U. Note the absence of a nose radar; and the MiG-19 'Farmer' in the background. (Tass)

99. This head-on view of the Yak-28P 'Firebar' clearly shows the lengthened nose cone, the missile launching shoes on the wing pylons, and the two wing-mounted Tumansky R-11 turbojets, each rated at 13,120lb st. (Tass)

100. The Yak-28 'Brewer-C' light bomber, few of which remain in Soviet service. Those that are in service have been converted for the reconnaissance or ECM roles. Note the open crew-door for the navigator forward of the canopy on aircraft '20'. (Tass)

▲99 ▼100

101▲

101. The first operational VTOL fighter in Soviet service is the Yakovlev Yak-36MP 'Forger-A', which was first identified when the aircraft carrier *Kiev* passed through the Dardanelles in July 1976. This official photograph shows the single-seat 'Forger-A' hovering over the deck of the *Kiev*. The engine layout of the 'Forger' is most unusual in that there are two vertical lift engines mounted behind the cockpit, and when in use the intake cover is raised (as illustrated); the other engine is a twin-nozzle vectored-thrust turbofan, with the nozzles mounted in the lower-rear fuselage. Because of this engine configuration, the 'Forger' cannot operate in the STOL mode, and so pays a penalty in payload/range for pure VTOL capability. (Tass)

102. The standard Yak-36MP 'Forger-A' fighter on the deck of *Kiev*, July 1979. Also shown here is an example of the two-seat 'Forger-B' training version (aircraft '04' in the photograph). The 'Forger' has no internal armament, but the two pylons under each wing are estimated to be capable of carrying 3,000lb (1,360kg) of external stores. (RAF)

102▼

▲103 ▼104

105▲

103. The Yakovlev Yak-18T shown in this photograph at the Paris air show in 1977 is a cabin-version of the Yak-18 'Max' trainer of the Soviet Air Force. It is used for pilot training, and has also been put into service as a liaison and ambulance aircraft. (MJG)
104. An L-39 Albatros of the East German Air Force, modified as a target tug. Note the winch fairing on the lower fuselage aft of the nose-wheel.
105. Czechoslovakia's Aero L-39 Albatros trainer succeeded the L-29 Delphin as the standard jet trainer of Czechoslovakia, East Germany and the Soviet Union in the mid-1970s. It entered Czech service in the spring of 1974, and by 1981 over 1,000 had been produced. This photograph shows the L-39C basic and advanced flying training version. The two other major variants are the L-39Z armed weapons trainer, which could have a war role of light strike and reconnaissance, and a similar armed version, the L-39ZO for export.

▲106 ▼107

106. With an aircraft industry of her own, Poland has developed her own jet trainer, the PZL-Mielec TS-11 Iskra. This photograph shows the export model of the range, Iskra-Bis D, during a visit to the Farnborough air show in 1978. Two of the five variants are single-seat light attack and reconnaissance models, in service with the Polish Air Force. (MJG)

107. Designed in the early 1970s, the IAR-93 Orao is a joint venture between SOKO in Yugoslavia and CNIAR in Romania. This twin-engined (Rolls-Royce Viper Mk.632-41 turbojets, each rated at 4,000lb st) ground-attack fighter made simultaneous first flights in the two countries on 31 October 1974. Some 200 aircraft are expected to be built for each country, and some 40 (including two-seaters) are understood to have been built to date. (via UK MoD)

108. Although not strictly a Warsaw Pact member, Yugoslavia does have a small, but flourishing aircraft industry – SOKO. During the early 1960s they developed a trainer and single-seat light strike aircraft. This photograph shows the single-seat J-1 Jastreb of the Yugoslav Air Force, powered by a Rolls-Royce Viper 531 turbojet, rated at 3,120lb st.

108▼

▲109

109. A line-up of SOKO G2-A Galeb trainers of the Yugoslav Air Force. Production began in 1963. The type has been exported to Libya and Zambia. The Galeb is powered by a Rolls-Royce Viper 11 Mk.22-6 turbojet, rated at 2,500lb st.

110. In the game of 'cat-and-mouse' played by the NATO and Soviet forces, interceptions are regular business for NATO interceptors. Indeed, several of the photographs in this book were taken on such occasions. This photograph shows a close-up of the tail of a Tu-95/142 'Bear', taken over the North Atlantic on 28 September 1980. The tail barbette turret housing a pair of 23mm NR-23 cannon and the radar above the turret are plainly visible. The universal sign from the observation window at lower right must surely supply the last words for this book. (USAF)

▼110